The Money Field

Book One

Nelson Letshwene

Book 1:

How to Set Your Own Money Rules

In the Game of Money, Everyone Is A Player, But Some Are More Skilled Than Others

Nelson Letshwene

Copyright© 2021 R. Nelson Letshwene, 2015, 2017

All rights reserved. This book is intellectual property protected by international copyright law. No part of this publication may be reproduced in any form without the prior written permission of the author and publisher, except in brief quotations embodied in critical articles and reviews.

Published by Moedi Publishing.
Gaborone, Botswana.
Pretoria, South Africa

©R. Nelson Letshwene
PO BOX 80927, Gaborone, Botswana
PO Box 1766 Rustenburg, 0323, South Africa
nelslets@gmail.com / nelson@moedi.net
Moedi Publishing
ISBN: 978-0-9870189-1-5

KDP ISBN:
ISBN-13: 978-1980564973

DISCLAIMER:

This publication is designed to provide competent and reliable general information regarding the subject matter covered. However, it is published with the understanding that the author and publisher are not engaged in rendering legal, financial, or other professional advice. If legal, financial, or other expert assistance is required, the services of a professional should be sought. The author and publisher specifically disclaim any liability that is incurred from the use or application of the contents of this book.

Other books by Nelson Letshwene: Books in The Money Field Series:

1. Book One: The Money Field - How To Set Your Own Money Rules
2. Book Two: Money Goals and Money Management Tools – Practical Strategies for Living in the Gap
3. Book Three: How to Pay Off Your Debts and Build Wealth – Avoiding The "Trap" of Other People's Money

To get access to other books by this author, Visit www.amazon.com/R-Nelson-Letshwene/e/B00Q4AEMCM/ref

Or Scan the QR Code on the next page

My amazon store is here:

People with wealth consciousness
settle only for the best.

Deepak Chopra

Nelson Letshwene

DEDICATION

For Lind'Okuhle and Nova

Table of Contents

INTRODUCTION TO THE SERIES xii
MAKING MONEY IS GOOD 1
1. INTRODUCTION TO PERSONAL FINANCE 5
2. DIMENSIONS OF PERSONAL FINANCE 9
3. AWARENESS, HONESTY, AND
RESPONSIBILITY 19
   THE TRIANGULAR CODE 20
   AWARENESS 22
   HONESTY 25
   RESPONSIBILITY 27
4. YOUR MONEY FIELD 33
   1. The Income Rule 37
   2. The Spending Rule 38
   3. Borrowing for consumption rule........................ 40
   The Repayment Rule 42
   5. The Budget rule or the "spending sheet" rule. 45
5. MONEY RULES FOR ASSETS BASE 49
   1. The Savings Rule 50
   2. The Return of savings rule 54
   3. The Money-In-Money-Out rule............................ 55
   4. The Borrow-For-Assets rule................................. 56
   5. The Repossession Rule 59
   6. The Surrender Rule 60
6. THE VALUE OF AN INCOME 63
   The Value of an Income 64
   Who takes my money before I do? 65

How often do you pay yourself? 66

7. CONSUMER BEHAVIOUR 71
The commercialization of our senses 72
FUNCTIONAL LITERACY 75

8. THE INTELLIGENT MONEY FIELD 79
1. The Pay Yourself First Rule 80
2. The Return on Savings Rule 82
3. The Balanced Split Rule 84
The Spider-Web Economic Doctrine 86

9. WHY IS IT DIFFICULT TO SAVE MONEY? 89

10. DEBT AND FINANCIAL INTELLIGENCE 95
Do Financially Intelligent People Borrow Money? 96
4. Borrowing for Security 97
5. Performing Assets Rule 100
6. The Positive Cash Rule 101
7. The Profit rule or Income from liabilities rule 103
8. The Sponsoring Rule 104
Does my Income exceed my Expenses? 106

11. POSITIVE CASH FLOW AND RE-INVESTMENT 109
9. The Re-Investment Rule 110
10. The Self-sustenance rule 112

12. FINANCIAL GOALS 117
Success Through Goal Setting 117
The Power of Writing Down Your Goals 120
Smart Goals 122

ACKNOWLEDGEMENTS 127

ABOUT THE AUTHOR 129

BIBLIOGRAPHY 131

RECOMMENDED READING..................................134

For Other Books by NELSON LETSHWENE....135

INTRODUCTION TO THE SERIES

The Kindle version of this book has been broken into a series of three books. This is the first instalment of the series.

This will cover the basic principles of *The Money Field*, defining and illustrating it as a field upon which the game of money is played. It covers all the rules that are applicable in the game of money, along with the players that you get to meet on *The Money Field*. On *The Money Field*, no one is ever alone. There are many players whose moves affect your own moves as in a game of chess. It is important to build your own winning strategy on your own Money Field. This first part in the series will help you in understanding and applying the rules to your own game, and will conclude with money goals. Once goals are set, there is a gap between where you start and where you desire to end.

The second book in the series will cover practical strategies for living in the gap. Many people fail to meet their goals simply because they fail to live in the psychological gap between where they start and where they wish to end their goals. This gap requires practical strategies that will be covered in the second book in the series.

The third part of the series focuses on what we call "Other People's Money", or simply Debt Management Strategies. This will cover tools of debt or debt instruments used by lenders to get their money into your pocket. You in turn need to have effective strategies to get their money safely back to them without any damage having been done to you. It is more beneficial to you if you use other people's money to your advantage rather than to have them use you to grow their money only. The third part will also cover the structure of debt and debt elimination strategies.

Some of the material in this book was formerly published in the paperback book *Functional Mastery Over My Finances* (Reach publishers, 2008). Although some of the chapters that formed that book are in this book, they have been revamped, improved, updated, edited and made better for the sake of this new book series; and many other chapters of that book have been excluded. This is therefore not necessarily a second edition of that book.

The reason for this new book series was to clarify and add more to some of the concepts that were discussed in that paperback book.

I have been blessed enough to "workshop" the material in this book series all over the country and the region.

Through these workshops I have met lots of people whose questions and concerns have helped to add more substance to this material and improve it.

In this book series I have also sought to encourage participation by including self-assessment questions at the end of each chapter.

I hope this book series will add value to the life of the reader, and help to increase financial literacy and other money skills that are so important in our lives.

If you enjoy this book series and find it helpful, and I hope that you will, I would appreciate a little feedback or brief review at your convenience.

Thank you,

Nelson Letshwene

Nelson Letshwene
April, 2021
Gaborone, Botswana
nelson@moedi.net

PREFACE

MAKING MONEY IS GOOD

"Opportunity is missed by most people because it is dressed in overalls and looks like work."
Thomas Edison

Money is a cornerstone of the human experience. We human beings have held and continue to hold dysfunctional beliefs about money. The time of change is now. Life was created for our enjoyment.

Money enables us to enjoy life. Money is not different from anything else in life – it is all energy, the energy of God, the omnipresent God, who fills all in all. There is no place God is not, including in money. To reject money is to reject something of life. To call money bad is to call energy bad.

Many people hold a dysfunctional view of

money. Dysfunctional in that it is not helping them. It is not 'working' for them.

They hold the view that money is evil, and they are good, and therefore they repel money.

For how can that which is good attract that which is bad? They make money wrong, dirty, and unworthy. They call the rich, "stinking rich"; they call money "filthy lucre". They talk of "obscene profits".

It is this very idea that makes those who do "dirty jobs" make a lot of money, while those who do "good jobs" go begging.

The preachers and teachers of our children, and the scientists looking for a cure for AIDS go begging for money for their good deeds, while the dancers and players are splashed with money. Our psychology on money is backwards. It is time to have a right-side up attitude towards money.

It is fitting that every human being lives luxuriously. The earth has enough resources that we should all live luxuriously.

We as a species have however not yet learnt how to make that work. We have created an imbalanced world of the rich and the poor; few rich people and a majority living in abject poverty; and that, on a planet with resources that can feed all its inhabitants abundantly.

This book is to take you to places where your disempowering beliefs will be challenged, and opportunities will be handed back to you.

It seeks to help you to feel good about making money. It will help you to have a healthy respect for money; to stop shunning that which gives you life.

It is time to joyfully accept money for the services you render to humanity. Indeed, it is time to joyfully accept all good things in life, and joyfully share with others. Be not ashamed of money, for money perpetuates life. Welcome it into your life and allow it to stay with you.

Use money. Share money. Give money. Receive money. Give it love and it will love you. Do not criticise it. Praise it for what it is able to do for you. Invite it into your life. Live a life of appreciation for all good things.

Making money is good. That which produces good is good. Love money for what money can do for you. Money gives you the ability to bring good to others. The good Samaritan wasn't broke! Mother Teresa, who did her good works among the poor wasn't broke! Yes, she was not greedy, but she was not broke! Her foundation is still bringing lots of good to the poor.

People may often say that money does not buy happiness; but haven't you noticed that when you have money you just seem to be a little happier than when you don't have it?

Nelson Letshwene

Chapter 1

1. INTRODUCTION TO PERSONAL FINANCE

> "This is not a game where the guy with the 160 IQ beats the guy with the 130 IQ."
> Warren Buffet

A life skill is practically a skill you should not go through life without. Personal Financial Management is a life skill! Why do so many people choose to go through life without mastering this skill?

You can "get away" with not having the skill to swim if your reason is that you stay too far from rivers and oceans, and that your country is land-locked. But how far can you run from money? Have you ever asked yourself any of these questions?

- Where did all the money go?
- Have you ever wondered why budgets don't work?

- Have you ever wondered why you seem to have lost control over your finances?
- Have you ever wondered why, no matter what you do, you don't seem to be balancing your finances?
- Are you starting to believe that indeed 'the rich get richer and the poor get poorer', and that's just the way it is?
- Are you starting to believe that indeed money is the root of all evil?

Where do all such beliefs come from?

Indeed, many people are uncomfortable in the presence of cash, that's why they'd rather spend it. Many believe that money is evil, that's why they get rid of it, albeit subconsciously. Personal Financial management is an essential life skill:

- It is essential for you.
- It is essential for your children.
- It is essential for your friends and family.
- It is essential for anyone who has ever asked: where did all the money go?

The primary purpose of this book series is to give you the essential skill of managing your personal finances. Many people are intimidated by the financial lingo. They therefore stay away from financial books and financial conversations. Do not be afraid. We present this material in a language you can understand. The fact is, everyone handles money, but not everyone is equipped with the skills necessary in handling money. Almost everyone uses credit, but not everyone is equipped to understand the language used by financial institutions and moneylenders.

Eliminate Your "I don't Knows"
The best way to understand this material or anything in life, is really to minimise your "I don't know's".

This allows you to begin making some decisions and see where they lead you. If you love your 'I-don't-knows', you will remain undecided, in which case you are likely to 'go with the flow'. But the truth is, you might not like where the flow is flowing to. An "I don't know", produces paralysis and fear.

So, the approach should be, "If I thought I knew the answer, what would it be?" While this approach does not say 'I know the answer', it gives you the opportunity to try different answers. It simply says, what if this was an answer, what effect would this have on the problem I am attempting to solve?

The problem of "right" and "wrong" answers exists only in schools. In real life, there are no "right" or "wrong" answers. There are events that produce outcomes. The reason schools have "right" and "wrong" answers is because they have to allocate marks and decide whether you have "passed" or "failed".

In the field of personal financial management, what is "right" for you may not necessarily be "right" for someone else. The answers are personal. Success is a personal thing.

Just as a disclaimer, we want to state here that no book can be a replacement for personal financial advice. Should you need personal advice, please utilise the services of a trained professional.

The field of personal finance is huge and no one book can cover all the material.

Welcome to this book series and I want to thank you for taking this precious opportunity to learn this ever-important subject of life.

Thank you.

Nelson Letshwene

Chapter 2

2. DIMENSIONS OF PERSONAL FINANCE

"An investment in knowledge pays the best interest."
Benjamin Franklin

> **LEARNING OUTCOMES:**
> In this chapter, you will learn to:
> - Identify the various dimensions of personal finance
> - Identify the seven essential money skills

Dimensions of personal finance represent various variables that influence people's relationship with money.

These variables are influenced by cultural, geo-political, economic, social, and personal preferences.

While there may be some general agreements among personal finance experts as to which behaviours would constitute what may be accepted as creating a more functional relationship with money, it remains the domain of each individual to determine what they do with their money.

The field of personal financial management covers a vast area of dimensions that are often neglected when dealing with the subject. The dimension of money, as depicted by the figure below, cover almost all areas of personal financial management:

DIMENSIONS OF MONEY

(Pie chart showing: Money Skills, The Money field, Psychology of Money, Consumer Behaviour, The Money Tree, Money Goals, Budgeting, Debt Management)

A brief description of each of the dimensions depicted in the dimensions of money diagram is included below. Going clockwise beginning with The Money Field:

1. *The Money Field*™ is what we define as a field of play upon which the game of money

is played. This field consist of different players playing the money game, and you are one of them. In fact, everyone who handles money is a player on the money field. This is obviously the title of this book and will be covered in details in the book.
2. *The Psychology of Money* covers our emotional involvement with money. Most people have a huge emotional body and it influences just about every decision they make. This also covers the beliefs we hold about money and how such beliefs affect our relationship with money. There is a whole book that I have devoted to this dimension called *The Psychology of Money – money follows the character of its owner*. (It should be published here soon – check amazon.com)
3. *Consumer Behaviour* is a subject that seeks to alert the consumer to their behaviours that leave them vulnerable to "sales tricks" or the attempts of marketers to get consumers to part with their hard-earned cash. As a consumer, it is vitally important to understand other players on the money field and how they affect your money. I have often said, unfortunately the only people who do not understand consumer behaviour are the consumers. It is vitally important to know your money's friends and foes.

4. *The Money Tree*™ seeks to contradict the saying that "money does not grow on trees", and go on to show wealth-building systems used by the wealthy to build wealth. The saying that money doesn't grow on trees is a metaphor to emphasise that making money is hard. However, if you understand wealth building systems, and you go about setting them up, you are essentially, "planting money trees". If any person would dare to plant such money trees, they too could reap the fruit of their labour. This subject is covered in detail in Book 2 of this series.
5. *Money Goals* is a dimension of personal finance that helps people to set financial goals and follow strategies to help them to reach their goals. The last chapter of Book 1 of this series is devoted to this subject.
6. *Budgets* are normally the only dimension people focus on when they think they are working on their personal finances. Unbeknown to many, they have left out a lot of dimensions that affect their finances. No wonder people conclude that budgets don't work. A budget is a tool that if used properly, could help the user to take charge of their finances. The chapter on Budgeting principles in Book 2 of this series will give some guidelines on this subject.

7. *Debt Management* includes the entire realm of Debt planning, tools of credit, lending and borrowing guidelines, debt management, and debt elimination systems. Book 3 of this series is dedicated to this important subject.
8. *Money Skills* is a huge dimension of personal finance as depicted by the diagram below:

MONEY SKILLS

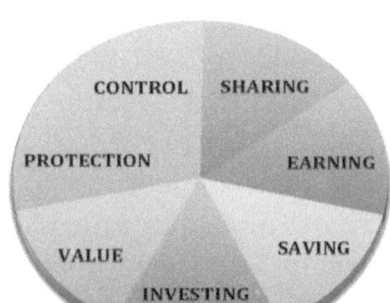

These Money Skills are essential for anyone who wants to take charge of their finances. Each one of these skills are like a computer software that must be "installed" in the brain for it to start working or to become part of a person's psychic behaviour. A brief description of each of these is listed below.

Going clockwise beginning with Earning:

1. *Earning* – this speaks of your ability to bring more money into your money field using your skills and talents. Most people

generally use only one main skill to bring money into their money field. They leave a lot of skills and talents "unemployed".

There are chapters in the second book of the series which will focus on Your Personal Money Tree and Marketing your Personal Skills.

2. *Savings* – Everyone knows the importance of saving, but not everyone is able to practice this skill effectively. There are a number of pitfalls that stop people from saving. These are covered in the chapter called Why is it difficult to save money. Saving is a very important first step in building wealth, and it is a very important skill to seek to master.
3. *Investment* – To invest is to put money away with an expectation of returns on your investments. Understanding the five investment systems and learning how to apply the learning practically is very important to mastering this skill. We will talk in this book about some of the processes necessary to implementing this skill on the money field.

In a separate book called *The Seven Essential Money Skills*, I cover all of these skills, and give more details to this particular skill.

4. *Value* – This skill speaks of your ability to create real value wherever you are. Understanding the time value of money and strategies that lead to growth is essential to mastering this skill. This is also an anti-waste skill. Learning to preserve your resources and not being wasteful leads to wealth accumulation and to growth. Many people are very wasteful, and therefore have to spend resources over and over again replacing today things that they bought yesterday. If they can only learn to preserve their resources, they would not have to spend new resources to replace them. A book called *The Millionaire Next Door* by Drs Stanley and Danko sheds greater light on the behaviours of millionaires who build wealth.

5. *Protection* – Many people are very vulnerable to financial pressures. They are so exposed that it takes very little events to destabilise their entire financial life. Protection speaks of your ability to mitigate the risks you are exposed to through insurance and the creation of legal entities. There practically isn't a risk that cannot be insured against. Many people, however, do not understand insurance products and are

therefore either under insured, or carrying wrong insurance products that don't apply to them.

Legal entities are tools used by wealth builders to protect their wealth. It has been said that the rich own nothing, but control everything, and this, through the use of legal entities.

6. *Control* – This speaks of your ability to take charge of your financial life. Control is divided into physical control systems and building emotional controls.

   In Book 2 of this series, we cover the paper trail, Physical arrangement of data and Creating Records. This is a focus on the physical control element of this particular skill. The emotional controls, as has been mentioned, will be covered in greater details in the book *The Psychology of Money*.

7. *Sharing* – This is an integral part of human behaviour. Learning to share your money and resources without guilt and obligations is the key to mastering this skill. Many people share from a "wrong" attitude and therefore don't get the real benefits of sharing. Learning how the rich create "giving systems" or philanthropies is one of the ways of mastering this skill.

SELF-ASSESSMENT:

1. Name and briefly explain the various Dimensions of Personal Finance covered in this chapter.

2. Name and briefly explain the Seven Essential Money Skills covered in this chapter.

3. Which of the Seven Money Skills would you like to learn more about?[1]

---

[1] Learn more in the book *Seven Essential Money Skills* by R. Nelson Letshwene. Also available in the Kindle Store or in paperback on amazon.com

Chapter 3

3. AWARENESS, HONESTY, AND RESPONSIBILITY

"Until you are willing to take responsibility for all of it, you cannot change any of it"
Neale Donald Walsch

LEARNING OUTCOMES:
In this chapter you will learn:
- The three core concepts of life
- How to be more aware of your behaviour with money
- How to be more honest with yourself about your true issues with money
- How to take more responsibility in taking charge of your finances.

Before we go on to engage The Money Field in the next chapter, it is important that we examine the three core concepts that can prepare us. These are represented by The Triangular Code.

THE TRIANGULAR CODE

What is the Triangular Code?
The three core concepts of life: Awareness, Honesty, and Responsibility, have been called The Triangular Code[2].
We will go into details about these three, but let us first look at them from the psychological perspective. In psychosocial systems the Triangular Code is represented by a triad:

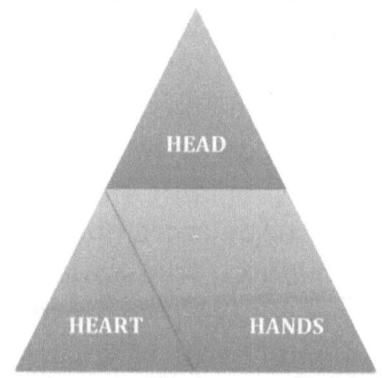

---

[2] Walsch, N.D, *Conversations with God*, Hodder & Stoughton

- AWARENESS, is a function of the HEAD.
- HONESTY, is a function of the HEART, and
- RESPONSIBILITY is represented by HANDS.
-

The HEAD represents awareness because it speaks of what you know about the subject at hand. It has been said that knowledge is power. I say what you don't know about money will hurt you.

When it comes to money, a lot of people don't *think* about money, but they *feel* about money! By skipping the head, your centre of awareness, and rushing to your heart, your emotions, you will be leaving an important part of your guiding system.

What makes us *act* before we *think*? It's the *emotions* from the heart! If you control your money with only your *emotions*, will you *act responsibly*?

If you *think* about your money more and increase your *awareness* about the subject, your emotions will be more controllable, which increases your level of *honesty*. The more honest you are about your money, the more responsible you become. Every responsible action you take also serves to increase your awareness, which continues to influence your emotions ... and the cycle goes on!

Money supports the character of its owner! We are here in large part not only to talk about money, but really to talk about its owner.

AWARENESS

What is awareness?
Awareness is what helps you to tap into your knowledge base. It is important before you comment on any subject to ask yourself honestly: what do you know about this subject? Are you making an informed decision or an emotional decision? Is this an educated decision or an ignorant reaction? How wide is your field of vision here?

Many people are sleepwalkers. They are unaware at a conscious level of what is happening in many areas of their lives, not the least of which is Personal Finance. Awareness leads to wakefulness.

This book seeks to bring you to a full awareness of what role money is playing in your life, how you can take control and make sure that you play the game as you choose. Awareness is the first step to this process.

> Have you ever gone to an ATM, withdrew money, and two days later wonder what happened to the money?

Most of us have. The time between the withdrawing of the money and the asking of the question, 'where did my money go?', is what I refer to as *'the awareness gap'*.

You have lost awareness if you can't answer that question. It's like you withdrew the money, fell asleep, then woke up two days later with an empty purse. You just can't remember what you did with the money.

For some people, the awareness gap is as long as five years, or ten years, or even more. This is the time when you stop, look at your life and ask:

- What have I done with my money all these years?
- What have I been working for?
- What has my money done for me?

Perhaps now is that time. Most people don't ever ask themselves those questions because they are afraid of the answers that they might get.

So, they prefer to remain unaware. They choose to stay asleep and never wake up. Now is the time to awake.

Give yourself all the facts, all the data about your life. Unless you give yourself all the facts, you are crippling your thinking process, and will therefore arrive at erroneous conclusions. For critical analysis to take place, you have to give yourself all the facts. You must be aware of what is going on. See things as they are, then you can make a decision to change them if they don't please you.

Bring yourself to full awareness:
- Are you aware of your habits and actions?
- Are you aware of your behaviours and emotions?
- Are you aware of your thoughts and your reasoning?

What habits and behaviours are propelling my money in the direction it is going? A habit is behaviour that you have done so many times that you don't have to think about it anymore. It has left the head; it is operated only from emotions and actions. There are various habits:
- Debt habits;
- Impulsive buying habits;
- Competitive habits;
- Saving habits;
- Investment habits; etc.

This question begins to tap on the root of the issue. Can you identify your habits?

HONESTY

Honesty speaks not only of truthfulness, but of integrity and openness. When I speak of truthfulness, I am not talking about you telling someone else the truth. In this instance, I am talking about you telling you the truth about you. If you can't disclose the whole truth to yourself, you have a bigger problem than you have imagined.

Integrity is the opinion you have of yourself. Not what you think others think about you, but what you are thinking about yourself. What is your opinion of yourself?

Here is an **Integrity test**: Answer yes or no.

PART 1:
1. Do you honour yourself?
2. Can you keep your own promises to yourself?
3. Can you say "no!" to harmful things to yourself?
4. Do you build yourself up?
5. Do you develop yourself?
6. Do you invest in yourself?
7. Are you growing?
8. Who are you?

PART 2
9. Do you sabotage yourself?

10. Do you always put yourself down and last?
11. Do you sacrifice yourself to try and please others?
12. *Do you spend money you do not have, to buy things you do not need, to impress people you don't even like?*
13. *Who are you?*

Count your "yes's" and your "no's". In the first part you should get as many "yes's" as possible, and in the second part you should get as many "no's" as possible.

For every "no" you got in the first part, figure out how you can correct that. For every "yes" you got in the second part, also, figure out how you can correct that.

Just remember that "the truth" does not exist as an objective reality. It is your truth you must always seek, not someone else's. Once you find your truth, don't try to compare it with the truths of others. Just live by your truth.

It is only when you are honest to yourself, and therefore become aware of your situation, that you can move on to the next step of taking responsibility. This is face-to-face with yourself! Can you face yourself? Literally! Can you stare at yourself in the mirror, eyeball to eyeball without getting uncomfortable with what you see? What are you going to do about what you are seeing?

You are hereby invited to meet yourself. Then you shall know yourself anew, like you have never known yourself before!
When you can feel compassion for yourself, then grace shall abound to fill your heart!

Honesty gives birth to openness. Openness of mind is the doorway to understanding and clarity. An open mind leads to light-heartedness that perceives no attack and therefore sees no need to be defensive.

"Nothing real can be threatened" ACIM[3] Your real self knows this, and therefore is afraid of nothing.

RESPONSIBILITY

Responsibility speaks not only of duty, but of accountability and conscientiousness. The duty in responsibility comes in recognising your role in the outcomes or the aftermath of your life. Accountability speaks of your recognition of how your actions affect others, while

---

[3] ACIM = A Course in Miracles. www.acim.org

conscientiousness speaks of your awareness in the entire process.

Responsibility means accepting the "blame" of it all. Not at all meaning that you should feel guilty – but knowing that you did it. Even if it was not all physically done by you, but that you had a role in it.

When you look at your situation, you will accept that you did it to yourself.

Sure, others may have contributed, but at the end, you did it to yourself. Perhaps it was in ignorance or unconsciousness, but still, when you awake, you realise that you did it to yourself. This is where you come to the realisation that, as Walt Kelly's comic strip character Pogo said:

"We have met the enemy, and he is us."

Another author put it this way:

"Until you are willing to take responsibility for all of it, you can't begin to change any of it[4]"

---

[4] Walsch, N.D. *Conversations with God*

Take a look at your finances. Who did it to you?
- Okay, the banks may have contributed;
- The moneylenders may have chipped in;
- Your relatives may have added something;
- Your employer may bear some responsibility;
- Your children perhaps?
- The government?
- The system?

But really, who did it to you?

Responsibility says, I have arranged the situations around me to produce the results that I now have.

As long as you keep blaming others, you take your own power away from you. You are saying there is nothing you can do because you are not the one producing the results that you are observing. That is really disempowering yourself.

Taking responsibility might include something as simple as deciding to remove yourself from the situation that depresses you.

When we talk about taking personal responsibility in the area of personal finance, it will surely include some actions on your part. It may include taking the responsibility to work harder and find other ways of increasing your income. It will call you to make some tough decisions. But you must remember that only you can do that.

You can't keep walking around with a "woe is me" attitude if you are ever going to change. You will have to get out of your self-pity party, clean up the mess of the party, and start afresh. A declaration such as "I can do it" sets a tone for a new beginning.

You say, here is my financial situation, and I now take charge! All I need is guidance. Show me the map, let me identify where I am, let me decide where I want to go, and let me take the first step!

- How can I make more money?
- How can I protect more of my money?
- How can I ensure that more of my money goes where I want it to go, that is how can I exercise more control?

Taking responsibility includes gathering information about yourself. You may start by asking:

"What is the source of my income?"

List all your regular sources of income and their frequency: Employment; Business; Dividends; Sales; Gifts; Other.

And, if you depend on borrowed money as income, also, list them. This allows you to see how much of other people's money you depend on: Loans; Overdraft facilities; Credit cards; etc.

> Many people are on a revolving credit system. You earn 10'000,00. You have a revolving credit from a credit card or overdraft facility of 5'000,00.
>
> You therefore *think* you live a lifestyle of 15'000,00. You are actually still living on 10'000,00 or less. Only in the first month when you used the "available credit" did your lifestyle go to 15'000. After that, you returned to 10'000. And now you are perpetually in debt to the tune of 5'000.
>
> At the end of every month, your account is at negative 5'000,00. Your salary of 10'000,00 comes in, fills up the hole and you have a positive balance of 5'000.00, and you spend the positive balance of 5'000,00; plus, the 5'000,00-revolving credit.
>
> The difference is of course that the additional 5'000,00 is borrowed money for consumption and it always comes at a cost. That cost reduces your lifestyle.
>
> If your salary should stop right now, you will remain in debt to the tune of 5'000 plus costs!

SELF-ASSESSMENT

1. What does Awareness mean to you?

2. What does Honesty mean to you?

3. Did you take the Integrity test? What elements of the test do you need to work on?

4. Are you a blame-shifter?

5. What will you do to take more responsibility in your finances?

Chapter 4

4. YOUR MONEY FIELD

"Money is only a tool. It will take you wherever you wish, but it will not replace you as the driver."
Ayn Rand

> LEARNING OUTCOMES
> In this chapter we introduce the following concepts:
> - The Money Field as a field of play
> - Different money rules as applied on the money field
> - How people get stuck in the debt cycle

There are different ways that people try to hold the idea of money in their lives. I use what I have come to call, "The money field™".

This field is made of the ingredients that almost everyone applies in their money game. I also see this as a game with rules. Our role is to understand the rules so that we can play the game and win. Look at this field and understand that you are already playing your money game on it, whether you know it or not.

Understanding the flow of money on this field is the goal of this book.

There are four basic quadrants on the field of money as depicted in the diagram below. Every single person on earth operates on this field of money: the rich, the poor and everyone in between alike.

THE MONEY FIELD

INCOME	EXPENSES
ASSETS	LIABILITIES

This is the field of money upon which everyone who's ever handled money plays according to certain rules that are not written down, but somehow, they get adopted and applied.

Our rules of money are affected by many different factors including our upbringing, social standing, geopolitical factors, economic factors, and the society in which we live. Most importantly, however, our money behaviour is influenced by the beliefs that we hold to be true for ourselves.

Below are the rules that we will apply on the money field:

1. The Income or Earnings rule
2. The Spending rule
3. Borrowing for consumption
4. The Repayment rule
5. The Budget rule
6. The Savings rule
7. The Return on savings rule
8. The Borrowing for assets rule
9. The Repossession rule
10. The Surrender rule

For the most part, we all start at the same point. We start with nothing, facing the empty field. We start playing the game as soon as we have an income.

Take an example from the game of soccer. The size of the soccer field is standardised by FIFA (Fédération Internationale de Football Association). All the rules are also set by FIFA. Any team anywhere in the world, whether professional or amateur, will play on the same standardised pitch, applying the same rules.
There are no different set, or, rules for professional soccer players. There is no different size pitch for amateurs.
When the referee blows the whistle for the games to begin, the most skilful players know exactly what they need to do from that moment to the end of the game.

But if you put an amateur team or children on the soccer pitch that do not know the rules, it is entertaining to see how they all just follow the ball wherever it goes without any apparent coordination. If one of them scores they all celebrate, even if it's an own goal.

The Money Field is also a static, but invisible field upon which the game of money is played. The four quadrants of the money field are governed by standard rules for all the players. The differentiating factor on the money field is the skill of the players. As the subtitle of this book says, in the game of money everyone is a player, but some are more skilled than others. Because the money field is largely invisible, most people have no clue at any given time which quadrant they are in, and what the applicable rules for that quadrant are.

In this book, we have created this visual, so that you can always know where you are and what you are doing. We are players on this field in the game of money. This game has no reserves or bench warmers. Everyone is in the field, playing their own game.

Some of us, when it comes to our money game, we are just like children on the soccer pitch. We do not know the rules so we just follow the money wherever it goes. Even when we score "own goals" we celebrate like children, until we are told that we have lost the game.

We celebrate when we get a personal loan and weep when we have to repay. We are reluctant to score real goals in building assets and love our quick fixes of quick loans.

Let us now spend some time learning some of the rules that are applicable on the money field. Let us observe our behaviour on the field and see whether we are winning the game. We will take each rule as it applies and see how we apply it in our games.

Let us begin.

1. The Income Rule

The first rule of money is the income rule. We all start at the point when money enters our field in the income quadrant. For most of us, that moment is when you receive your first income. At that moment, it's like the referee has just blown the whistle for the games to begin. It is reflected as arrow number 1 in the money field below (Figure A). Now the games can begin.

Figure A

INCOME → 1	EXPENSES
ASSETS	LIABILITIES

The Income Rule is important because without it, the game cannot begin in earnest. This income may be your salary or wages, it may be a gift or allowance.

What do you do when you receive your first income? Most people just do what is the most normal thing for them. Normalcy is a factor of our perception. We often do what we have seen other 'normal' people around us do.

We have earned our money and we feel proud. Now it's time for the next rule in our money game.

2. The Spending Rule

For many of us, the first thing we do, the next rule of money we apply is that when money comes in, money must go out.

This is the second arrow marked (2) in the

money field below (Figure B). It is reflected in the expenses quadrant of the money field. You have now moved money from the income quadrant, to the expense quadrant, and it is never coming back!

Figure B

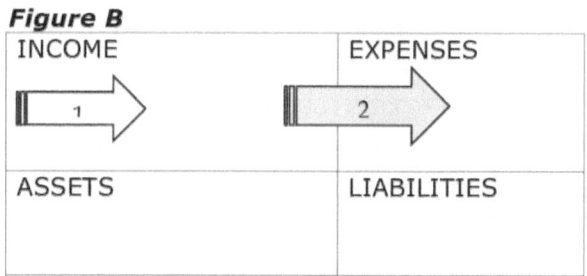

The Spending rule, or The Money-In-Money-Out rule is a rule applied by many people all over the world. It is fuelled by many different needs, wants, and beliefs about money. Marketers are working hard to get people to apply this rule through advertising and promotions. Politicians want people to spend in order to "boost" the economy. As popular as the Spending rule or money-in-money-out rule is, unfortunately, for some people, that is where they get stuck. That is the only rule they ever learn. They know that when money comes in, money must go out.

If this is the only money rule you know, it does not matter how much money is coming in. As much as comes in, must go out.

Not Enough!
The trouble with the Spending rule is that man is a growing being with growing needs and desires. As he gets used to spending for stuff, he desires more and more stuff. The trouble is that the income is not growing at the same pace with desires.

You are now experiencing the "not enough-ness" of money. This creates a problem. Since we are natural problem solvers, we look around us to see how other people have solved this problem, and we start to emulate them.

We learn the next rule of money. Our intention is not to get into trouble, but to solve the problem of "not enough-ness" or the problem of lack.

3. Borrowing for consumption rule

We now start to involve Other People's Money (OPM) in our money game. We look at the field and say, which quadrant has idle money? Low and behold, another player on the field, the lender, has already spotted you, and offers to solve your problem. This seems very harmless. Besides, many other fellow players on the field have utilised this strategy of solving the problem of not enough-ness.

This is the rule that includes the next quadrant in your money field. The focus of the Borrowing-For-Consumption rule is intended to increase your income so that you can effectively carry out the Spending rule or the Money-In-Money-Out rule. You go to the lender; you fill out the forms and the next day your lender calls you and says 'your loan has been approved'.

If you are like most people, you get excited because it seems your income has grown overnight, and now you can afford the things you couldn't afford the day before.

It is represented by the arrow (3) moving from the liabilities quadrant to the income quadrant in the field in figure C.

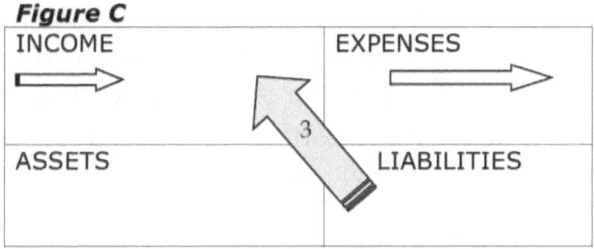

Figure C

You have just temporarily increased your income by borrowing.

By the way, your lender told you that you are special. To qualify for this rule in the formal sector, it is imperative that you have an income

– a salary. Many people get very excited when they are told that now they "qualify" to apply this money rule in their game.

Not everyone can apply this rule in their money game, at least not in the formal sector, although many people apply it informally, and the consequences are almost the same as in the formal sector, if not worse. When the lender calls and says you now qualify for a loan, it's as if you have achieved a milestone in your life.

This Borrowing-For-Consumption rule comes in various forms. Generally, it's in the form of a personal loan, a credit card, an overdraft facility, or a store card, or even hard cash from the lender in the form of a cash loan.

Before you introduced this rule in your life, you were pretty much playing the money game by your own money and your own rules to some extend. As soon as you learn and apply the Borrowing-For-Consumption rule, you are involving other people or entities in your money game, and they too come with their own rules, which you must now accommodate in your life. This is when you find out the next rule:

The Repayment Rule

All money borrowed must be repaid! This rule

introduces new movement of money on your field. While you were filling in the forms at your lender's office, they informed you about this new rule, but you did not hear them, – well, you heard them but it did not register. What was important to you at the time was getting more money.

To qualify for the Borrowing-For-Consumption rule, you must prove that you are able to apply its companion rule, the Repayment rule. That is why qualifying for a loan or a credit card seems to be such an achievement for many people.

Of course, the Repayment rule does not come into play until a month or in some cases, even three months later. So you don't feel its impact until the time to apply it comes in.

All loans create expenses through interest, and of course the repayment of the principal. On the field below (figure D) it is represented by arrow (4), which indicates a new expense that supports or feeds the liability.

Figure D

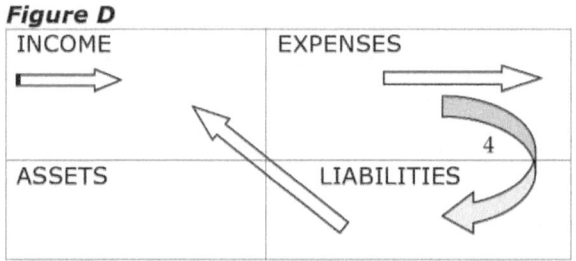

By the time of the application of the Repayment

rule, you start to realise that really, your income alone is not enough. Here, a lot of people get stuck. They have learned only four money rules and they think that's all there is to the game of money. They get stuck in a cycle.
- Money in, money out; not enough, borrow, and repay!

This is a new song that many people sing all the way to the grave.

"Money in, money out, not enough, borrow, and repay!"

The repetition is based on the fact that people don't take one loan and learn from it. They take one loan, then another, then another, without realising that they are not making any progress on their money game. They are repeating the same move over and over again. They even take loans to repay loans!

This is like the treadmill at the gym. You are running and you are getting tired but you are going nowhere. Many people spend a lifetime playing the money game by only these few limited rules. This does not apply to individuals only. Many companies, of course run by individuals who only understand these few rules, run their companies like they run their lives. Money is going out faster than it is coming in.

At this stage many people try to introduce other financial tools to try to help them. The only problem is that even these financial tools are not properly understood and so their applications seem fruitless. One of the first financial tools often applied is a tool called a Budget.

5. The Budget rule or the "spending sheet" rule

This rule at this stage should be called the Misapplied-Budget rule, or more aptly, The Spending-Sheet-Rule.
While a budget can be a truly freeing financial tool, when it is misapplied, it becomes a very restricting tool and many people don't like it.
We use a 'budget' to try to reduce our spending and to restrict our life-styles. What we call a budget is really a Spending Sheet.
At the end of every month, we look at what remains of our income after everyone else, including the government, have taken their share, and we draw up a sheet that will determine what we should do with the balance. It's like you have cooked this pot of food, dished out for everyone else, and now you have to live on the leftovers, if any.
We notice that money is going out faster than

it is coming in and we are seeking to plug the holes of the apparently sinking ship, but we can't seem to be able to bail the water out fast enough. This Budget that was supposed to help me is only serving to restrict me and limit me. I am not happy.

We are freedom-seeking beings and we don't like it when our lives are restricted. The nature of a human being is to seek expression, not restriction.

After a while of budgeting and fidgeting, and getting frustrated, we toss the budget out because as far as we are concerned, it does not work. Most of us return to the rules we know, including the borrowing for consumption rule, and we continue to sing the same old song we have sung before!

This game seems to be unconquerable! There is an underlying problem in this money game.

What is it? What is it? (The budget rule has no representation on the money field since it's just about organisation and planning, and not moving money).

SELF-ASSESSMENT

1. Name and give a brief description of each of the five money rules learnt thus far in this chapter.

2. How does "not enough-ness" affect your money game?

3. What is the "song" sung by most people that are stuck in the money game?

Chapter 5

5. MONEY RULES FOR ASSETS BASE

"Financial peace isn't the acquisition of stuff. It's learning to live on less than you make, so you can give money back and have money to invest. You can't win until you do this."
Dave Ramsey

LEARNING OUTCOMES
In this chapter you will learn:
- Why saving seems fruitless
- The borrowing for asset rule
- The repossession and the surrender rule

We have been introduced to the money field and have started to notice how easy it is to formulate money habits. We just allow money to come and go without some apparent controls on our part. We have seen the weakness of our problem-solving systems. Let us continue to see some of the things we do on the money field.

As you get along in years, you realise that you really can't live like this any longer. You have to find something that will help you. This is when you really start thinking about the next rule in the money game:

1. The Savings Rule

You have always known about savings and how important they are. In fact, your salary may even be received into a so-called Savings Account. The only problem with this so-called savings account is that it comes with an ATM (Automated Teller Machine) card that also has buying capabilities.

Whatever you have put in that account, every time you see an ATM, it seems to have a magnetic ability to draw you to it, and it makes you withdraw money. Every time you enter a store, there is a swiping machine there for your convenience.

I think this account should be called a Spending Account. After all, that's all it ever seems to be able to do for you.

Now you start to realise that you have to have either a separate real savings account where you can put something aside, or devise some other means of saving money.

You make a decision to save money. But, to save money, something has to give. You either have to cut back on some of your expenses, get out of debt, or find a way to generate more income.

Finally, you decide to join a savings club, a stokvel or "motshelo", where every month the members commit to put something aside as a saving. Or you just go to your bank and open a savings account.

This introduces a new route on your money field. For the first time, something starts going into your Asset quadrant.

This is indicated by arrow (5) in your money field (Figure E).

Figure E

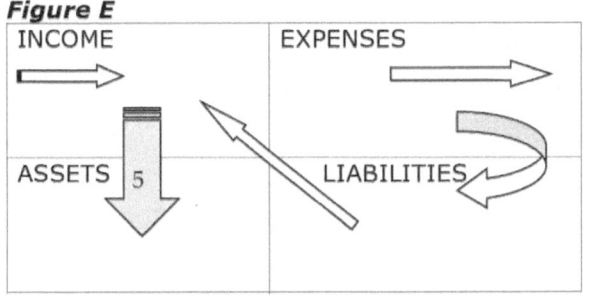

Saving money takes many forms for many of us. There is long-term savings and short-term savings. For many of us, long-term savings, even though we may participate in them, are far removed from us and it therefore seems that they do not exist because we don't see the money.

This is the pension or retirement fund that gets deducted from our salary before we see it. Some of us have taken a life insurance policy or an insurance savings policy. These long-term products don't always play on the field in our daily money game.

The visible savings-rule comes into play when we are saving for a particular thing in our lives like a piece of furniture, a vehicle, or a holiday. There are other forms of savings that we engage in.

Some are formal through financial institutions, and others are on a more informal fashion as mentioned above. These include social programs such as what we call Stokvels or "Motshelo".

Under these social savings programs, a group of us gather together on a monthly basis and we put a certain agreed amount into a fund. This fund is usually put into a savings account and our commitment is that each member should contribute every month.

The operation of these programs has evolved

over time. In their original fashion, they were for saving for a whole year and then dividing up the money at the end of the year and starting over again the following year. The evolution of these funds now includes lending money to their members over the year and charging them an interest. This is meant to increase the fund so that at the end of the year there is more to divide among the members.

There is no real advantage when only members borrow and charge themselves interest. The real advantage is when these funds lend to non-members and charge them interest. In this way the members of the fund will benefit from the outside source of income, which serves to increase each member's share at the end of the year.

Regulators are constantly watching to make sure that these social schemes don't turn into loan sharks as well.

They seek to restrict the lending and borrowing action to happen only among the members.

Since many people stuck in the life-style debt cycle as shown in the previous chapter, many members come back to these funds to continue their borrowing life cycle, and may be unable to repay, and at the end of the year, they would really have nothing left in the fund. The money-in-money-out system is very strong.

2. The Return of savings rule

With the Savings-Rule we come to realise that there is another rule at work called, Money-Saved-Comes-Back rule, or simply, the Return on Savings.

This, as we mentioned, may be at the end of the year when the fund is divided among members, or when a savings policy matures.

This introduces new flow on the money field and is indicated by arrow (6) in the money field below (Figure F).

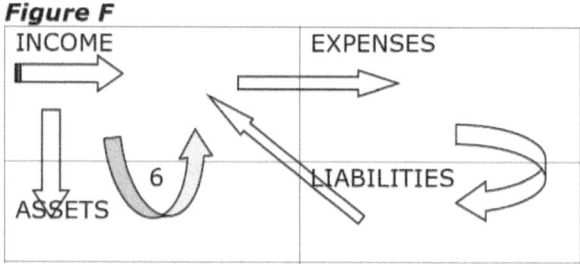

Figure F

This is money from your assets - (a savings account or fund) - into your income quadrant.

When money comes back to you from your savings, what you do with it depends on your psychology of money, and how the other rules are playing on your money field.

For most of us, as soon as money comes back into our income quadrant, the first rule automatically kicks in: Spend!

3. The Money-In-Money-Out rule.

The old habits kick in, we continue with our old life pattern and money rules. This is indicated by arrow (7) in the field below (Figure G).

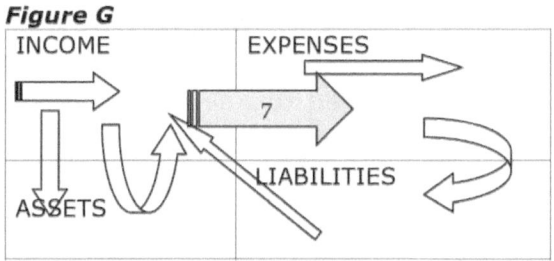

As you can see, arrow 7 is not really a new movement of money on the money field. It is just a repetition of the old Money-in-money-out rule. This can be a very frustrating time for many of us.

We have played just about all the money rules we know in the money game, but still, we are going nowhere.

We have worked for years, we have tried to budget, we have borrowed, we have saved, but we are still going nowhere. We accept this as how life is.

At this stage we have already formed many beliefs about money because of our experience. We know what works and what doesn't work, generally, we seem to know that nothing works.

How then does anyone get anywhere in this life? At this stage, beliefs like, "You can't live without debt" are cemented. You are getting along in years. The game doesn't stop. It must go on. You have been working for many years now. You have earned many salaries over the years but you still feel like you have nothing to show for it. You need to have at least a house of your own. A new rule must come into play on your money field.

4. The Borrow-For-Assets rule

You feel the need to own a real asset. Your own salary is never going to do it, so you do what everyone is doing. You go down to your local bank to apply for your first mortgage. Since you are still gainfully employed, and your rental can now be diverted to your mortgage, you qualify, and the new rule comes into play.

The borrowing for asset rule is a variation of the borrowing for consumption rule. The difference is that when you borrow for consumption, it is often in the form of unsecured loans, credit cards, or store cards, whereas, when you borrow for an asset like a house or a piece of immovable property, you have something more tangible to show for your loan.

This is the Borrow-for-Asset rule and the field starts to look like this, with the new rule represented by arrow (8) on the field (Figure H):

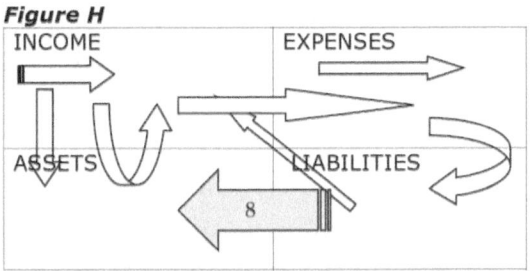
Figure H

However, just like the Borrow-For-consumption rule, the Borrow-for-Asset rule works hand in hand with the Money-Borrowed-Must-Be-Repaid rule. For most of us, our overcommitted salary remains responsible for the repayment of this loan. Every loan creates an expense.

As the repayment rule kicks into play, the field looks like this, with the new repayment represented by arrow (9) on the field (Figure I):

Figure I

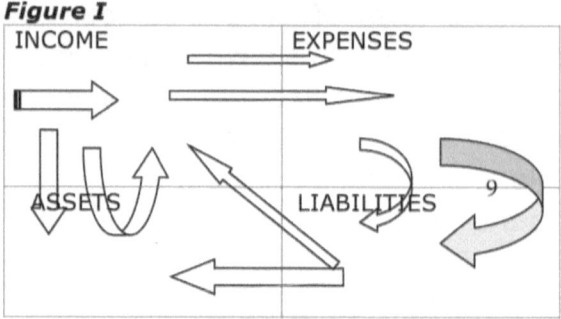

As you can see, arrow number 9 is not new.
It is a repetition of the old repayment rule. All money borrowed must be repaid. We've been here before. Are we making progress or going around in circles? As you can see, it's crowded on the money field. There are arrows going every which way. Many people go through life with this kind of money field. And this is called normal life. Based on this kind of money field, we build our beliefs about life. Millions of people live in the financial red line.

Many people reach retirement living from pay-cheque to pay-cheque, and they are forced now to live according to their 'budgets' because now they have no more strength to keep earning money to continue these rules on the money field.

In a worst-case scenario, other people get to experience other rules on the field. Another rule that other people get to experience in their lives, and more and more on an increasing scale, is the repossession rule.

5. The Repossession Rule

This rule is born of the Money-Borrowed-Must-Be-Repaid rule. Anyone who fails to obey the Repayment rule gets to experience the Repossession rule.

The repossession rule of course means that "your assets" go back to your creditors. This is represented by arrow (10) in the money field (Figure J)

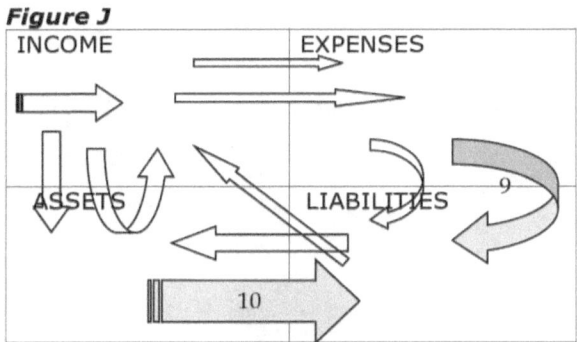

Some of us, realising where we are, and being unable to move on, we apply another rule called the Surrender rule.

6. The Surrender Rule

The surrender rule is when we start selling off our own assets just to try to increase our income to live on. The flow on the money field is the same as with the Repossession Rule.

In both cases, assets are leaving our assets quadrant.

When money leaves our asset quadrant, our net worth goes down, all in an attempt to increase our income.

Now the entire field of play looks like this (Figure K):

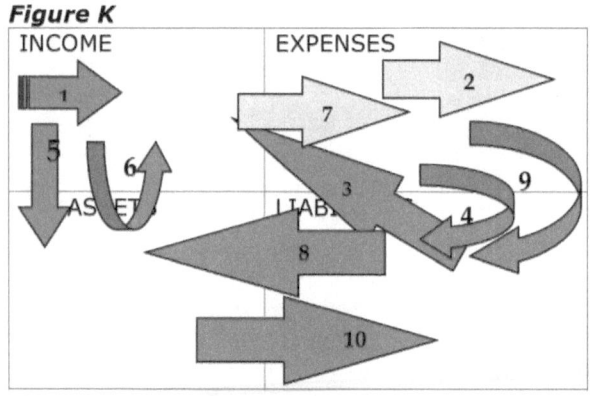

All the arrows from 1 to 10 represented.
1. The Earning Rule
2. The Spending Rule
3. The Borrowing for Consumption Rule

4. The Repayment Rule
5. The Savings Rule
6. The Return on Savings Rule
7. The Spending Rule (again)
8. The Borrowing for Assets Rule
9. The Repayment Rule (again)
10. The Repossession or Surrender Rule

This is the bleeding money field. Many people live in the financial red line. In the next chapter, we will focus on a different money field.

What could we do if we played this game intelligently? What are the different moves that the financially intelligent people do on the money field?

SELF-ASSESSMENT

1. Name and give a brief description of each of the Money Rules learnt in this chapter thus far.

2. What is the benefit of borrowing for assets?

3. How do the Repossession rule and the Surrender rule differ or overlap?

Chapter 6

6. THE VALUE OF AN INCOME

"It's not the employer who pays the wages. Employers only handle the money. It's the customer who pays the wages."
Henry Ford

> LEARNING OUTCOMES
> In this chapter you will learn:
> - The value of an income
> - Pay yourself first

People who play the money game intelligently seem to be playing by a completely different set of rules. In this chapter I would like you to consider the rules that can be helpful in winning the game.

Some of them, you may already be convinced that they don't work, but perhaps considering a new way of applying old rules can bring different results.

Before we look at the money field specifically and to understand the new rules, let us consider some things that are very important.

The Value of an Income

The wise have observed that often you don't value something until you lose it. Anyone who's ever lost a job knows the value of a job.

A job is the way most people make their living. However, increasingly we see that as the world population increases, shrinking industries can't keep up with the demands for new jobs, and therefore more and more people stay unemployed. This must lead to the rise of entrepreneurship, because whether employed or not, people will still demand goods and services. To be able to be an effective player in the money game, it is important that one has an income. An income is not only as a result of a job, but any commercially viable activity. An income creates possibilities.

If you have a source of income, it is important to value it, and not waste it. Stay positive, work with what you have and then enter the field.

We all start at the same point, whether financially literate or not. We start with an income whether from a job or from entrepreneurship, or as gift or inheritance. As was illustrated before, it is represented by the first arrow (1) in the field (Figure L).

Figure L

INCOME → 1	EXPENSES
ASSETS	LIABILITIES

For most people, when money comes into their money field, it creates emotions.
If left unchecked, these emotions will give direction to the money. The question would be, what would a financially intelligent person do when they receive money?

Who takes my money before I do?

Before we introduce the first rule of a financially literate person, let us honestly consider the following questions and their answers:
1. How often do you pay your landlord or mortgage company? (Every month?)
2. How often do you pay your electricity company? (Monthly?)
3. How often do you pay your water company? (Monthly?)

4. How often do you pay your telephone company?
    a. Your cellular phone companies?
    b. Your land-line company?
    c. Your Internet service provider?
5. How often do you pay your grocery store?
6. How often do you pay your fuel station?

It is obvious to all of us that these are the institutions or people we pay on a very regular basis. They seem to be the providers of our most basic needs, and therefore seem to deserve our money. When money comes in, we think of them first.

Is that how a financially intelligent person should think? What options do they have? Well, the financially intelligent start with a different question. Let us pose this question to you and see what your answer is:

How often do you pay yourself?

What is your honest answer to that question? "Pay myself? How can I pay myself?" That is the most frequent answer I get when I ask that question.

Most people are stunned by this question, because they assume that just because the salary comes in their name, it is theirs. And yet they pass it on to everybody else, and they are left with nothing.

Or, they pay everybody else, and whatever remains, if any, they get to keep. This is the exact mentality that keeps people in the financial red line. Another frequent answer to the question is: "I pay myself when I spoil myself!"

I ask, what do you mean by spoiling yourself?

"I take myself out to fancy restaurants, or buy myself nice things that make me happy" I ask, how much money comes to you when you do that?

Then they realise, money doesn't come to me, it leaves me, but it leaves me happy, they argue. Then I ask, if it left you, did you pay yourself, or did you pay someone else?

Who else takes your money before you do?
Are there predators on your money's path? From your employer or your clients to you, who has access to it before you do?

Have you set up systems to allow people access to your money?

Not everyone who has access to your money before you do is a predator. Some are good

guys like your Retirement contribution, because that's still money belonging to you.
Some are of course predators that once they have your money, you will never see it again.
Even if you have cash in your hand, consider that when you deposit it in an account, there will be a predator called, 'cash deposit fee'. If you withdraw money, there is 'withdrawal fee'. (Don't forget about these little invisible guys)
So list the beneficiaries and the predators on your money's path. Look at your pay slip and you will know.

Discomfort in the presence of cash?
Most people are cash avoiders! Have you noticed that about yourself? You might say, how can I be a cash avoider?
It sounds silly, doesn't it? But yes, most people are against cash, that is why they'd rather spend it.
Have you noticed that the institutions and people we listed above wants cash but you? They demand cash from you, and that is why you pay them first.
You, however, seem to prefer stuff. As soon as you hold cash in your hands, you want to exchange it for 'stuff'.
You are eager to get rid of it. When you have cash, you can't sit still. You want to go out and spend it. That is what we mean by saying that

you hate cash.

Many people are literally uncomfortable in the presence of cash. By getting rid of cash you are getting rid of the tools you need to play the money game.

Cash is the most important tool in the money game. To play the game, you need to have cash. Without cash, you can't play the game. Some try to play with borrowed money, but as we have seen, borrowed money plays by its own rules. To effectively play this game you need to practice the first rule of money. In the next chapter, we will look at the first rule of a financially intelligent person.

SELF-ASSESSMENT

1. What does it mean that people take your money before you do?

2. Who takes your money before you do?

3. What does it mean to pay yourself first?

4. What does it mean to be uncomfortable in the presence of cash?

5. What is the value of an income?

Chapter 7

7. CONSUMER BEHAVIOUR

"It is your "Attitude", not your "aptitude", that will determine your "Altitude"!"
Zig Ziggler

> LEARNING OUTCOMES
> - Important questions about consumers
> - The commercialisation of our senses
> - How to restore functional literacy

Why do the ordinary people play the money game the way that they do? Who taught them to play that way? Who said to them, as soon as you receive your money, you must spend it in a hurry?

Who said to them, if you run out of money, you should just borrow it?

How come people borrow money and seem to stay disconnected from the fact that they have to repay way more than they borrowed?

Why is it that most people don't see the addictive trap of borrowed money?

How come they find themselves ensnared until it's too late? Why do they think they can get out of debt by borrowing more money?

Who said to them that debt consolidation or debt restructuring is equivalent to debt management?

Who sawed these seeds of confusion?

If we can all sit down and begin to answer all of these questions, perhaps we can begin to understand consumer behaviour. Let us take a moment to understand ourselves. How do the other players influence our personal money game on the money field?

The commercialization of our senses

The senses. All five of them. Given to humanity to navigate rugged planet earth. Before we evolved, they were larger than life. Big ears, big eyes, big hands, open nostrils and a rough tongue to handle uncooked diet. Then we evolved.

Being presentable was redefined and beauty took over. Make-up for the eyes, nose jobs, hair to cover large ears, manicure, pedicure, and creams for the soft touch effects, and redefined job for the tongue. We may have forgotten our origins and the power of our senses, but commerce never forgot.

We are still largely motivated by our senses. They get us to act without much thinking. More often than not, our senses overcome our thoughts. You have a well-constructed, well thought out budget plan, but when you enter the shopping mall, your senses take over the shopping experience, and out goes your budget plan.

Any shopping mall you enter, there is a call to one or more of your senses. Your ears pick up sound waves of music that remind you of way back when ... and a desire to acquire that piece is activated, for posterity, of course! Mind you, the entire music industry would not exist if you did not have ears!

The perfume shop around the corner assaults your sense of smell and remind you of your lover, while the aroma from the food court activates hunger pangs that were otherwise asleep. Without your nose, the whole perfume industry would not exist.

The seemingly invisible blended colours make the mall seem natural while they activate the buying instincts within you. If you did not have eyes, colour would not matter.

The mood is just right, the music soft and appealing, the air filled with the scent of newness. You are invited by the sales person to just try it on, or just touch, which activates your sense of touch and make you feel good. You couldn't possibly put it down, could you?

The sales person might think you are broke, and we wouldn't want them thinking that now, would we? Out comes the credit card and whoosh! Impulsive buying has been activated. Who can stop it now?

Finally, you succumb to the hunger and you sit down to feast your eyes on the colourful menu that gets you to salivate even before you order your food. Of course, there are unplanned starters to get you started. Would you like to pre-order your desert? It's Crème brûlé! Before you know it, you are full and you are asking for the doggie bag to make room for the desert! Why did you ever order so much food when you were really not that hungry? Who is in charge? Your mind or your senses? Do you think or do you feel?

The goal of commercialization is to get you to feel more; to follow your senses; to forget about your thoughts. Let the chemicals flow in your veins! Only afterwards, when the bill from the credit card company comes, do you plead with your head to think of a plan to get you out! Again, we ask, who is in charge here?

FUNCTIONAL LITERACY

Functional ***illiteracy*** is high even in first world countries that have a 100% literacy rates. According to the Barbara Bush Foundation for Family Literacy[5], fully 27% of all American adults are "<u>functionally illiterate</u>".

In simple terms, this means, if supermarkets were to close down, these people would not know what to do to survive. That is functional illiteracy. Financial literacy is one of the pillars that can promote functional literacy.

The management of personal finances is vital in creating solid citizens who are in turn able to manage not only their own affairs, but the affairs of corporations, NGO's and government departments.

When managers are unable to manage their own personal affairs, they cannot realistically be expected to manage the affairs of corporations and organisations.

We have also come to realize that in addition to functional and financial strategies that are missing, one of the greatest contributing factors to financial illiteracy is the dysfunctional

---

[5] Hartmann Thom, *The Last Hours of Ancient Sunlight*, Three Rivers Press, NY, 2004

psychology of money.

Life skills and coping strategies are some of the things that can increase functional literacy. The promotion of emotional intelligence can build stable societies that are able to solve day-to-day problems and be able to project future solutions.

Functional behaviour is that which allows an individual to prosper in life by:

- Setting personal and financial goals
- Functionally "living in the gap" and moving towards meeting financial goals
- Behaving in a way that supports their financial goals and values
- Upholding functional and supportive money beliefs
- Keeping good personal financial records
- Being well informed in order to take appropriate financial decisions at critical times
- Being financially protected and not vulnerable to immitigable risks
- Keeping healthy relationships with other people in relation to money
- Living within and expanding their means
- Building a healthy nest egg for retirement

SELF-ASSESSMENT

1. Which industries depend on which parts of our senses?

2. How can consumers be more aware of how their senses are being commercialised?

3. What is functional illiteracy?

4. How can financial literacy improve functional illiteracy?

Chapter 8

8. THE INTELLIGENT MONEY FIELD

"If you don't change direction, you may end up where you are heading"
Lao Tzu.

> LEARNING OUTCOMES
> In this chapter you will learn:
> - How the wealthy apply money rules on the money field
> - The importance of the Pay Yourself First rule
> - The Balanced Split Rule
> - The Spider Web Economic doctrine

How do financially intelligent people play their money game? What are the most important rules that they follow? How do they keep their emotions in check? Who do they choose to involve in their money game? Who do they avoid on the money field? Who is in their team? What does it take to be a financially intelligent player?

1. The Pay Yourself First Rule

The Pay-Yourself-First rule is the most important rule in building financial stability. The application of this rule is the first step in the right direction, regardless of where you are in your life right now.

Even if you are currently living in the financial red line, your hope of escape is the Pay-Yourself-First rule. This rule starts to change the direction of money. Instead of starting with expenses, you start with your assets. This is represented by arrow (2) in the field below (Figure M):

The Pay Yourself First rule was popularized by George Clason in his 1926 classic, *The Richest*

Man In Babylon. In the book, the richest man teaches his students this rule:

> "A part of all you earn is yours to keep!"

His idea is that whatever money comes to you from whatever source, you must keep some for yourself! You must start building your asset base! He reckons your target should be 10%.

Until you learn <u>to keep</u> money, you have no hope of employing money for growth. You can't gainfully employ someone else's money. It can only work for them. You must learn to keep and employ your own.

How Do You Pay Yourself First?
Many people look at what they earn and how much they have to spend and they immediately know the answer to that question. It is impossible! How can I pay myself first when what I have is not even enough for me to live on? That is indeed a very important question and it will be answered later on as the pages roll on.

But the quick answer is that the reason for instituting the pay yourself first rule now is to try to create a new habit in your life. Many of us do not have the right habits when it comes to dealing with money.

Now, without worrying about the amount right now, ask yourself: have you established a savings habit? If not, this is the main reason for this rule.

George Clason recommends 10% of all that comes to you. Even if you can't afford 10% right now, you need to institute a habit of saving, with 10% as your target. Work at it until you are able to save at least 10%, and then work to increase that if you can.

Consider the idea that your current money habits may not be helping you, and you need to start new habits, one at a time.

For most of us, the only source of income that we have is our employment.

The Pay-Yourself-First rule introduces the concept of employing a resource called money, and this rule brings into play the Money-Saved-Comes-Back rule that we looked at earlier.

In the next chapter we will focusing or dealing with some of the obstacles to saving.

2. The Return on Savings Rule

Saved money has a potential to earn you more money in the form of interest. If invested well, it can also bring back dividends and profits.

You will never earn interest, dividends, or

profits until you learn to pay yourself first.
On the money field (figure N), this is indicated by arrow (3), money coming back into your income quadrant from your asset quadrant.

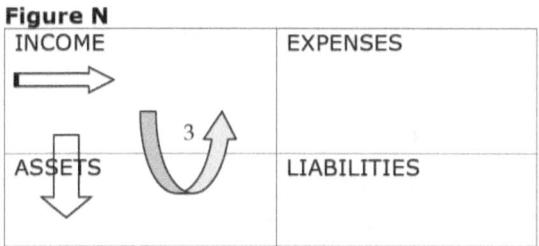

Figure N

Money saved comes back in its totality as well as in the form of interest or other forms of returns on investments (ROI).

In other words, money saved in a proper way never comes back alone. The principal always comes back with a return. I'm not talking about speculative investments.

It is important to take the Pay-yourself-first rule seriously because in it lies the hope of success. This rule, although a natural rule of increase, is unknown or disregarded by a lot of people.

If you have not yet read George Clason's *The Richest Man in Babylon,* I recommend that you read it to begin to build some financial literacy. In that book are some rules of money that are very helpful in building financial intelligence.

How does a Financially Intelligent person utilise their money?

3. The Balanced Split Rule

The Balanced Split rule says, when money comes in, instead of immediately applying the Money-in-Money-Out rule, rather think about some money staying in your income quadrant, some going to the Asset quadrant, and some going to your expenses quadrant.
If you learn to keep just 10% of your earnings, 90% remains for you to play your expense game.

The balanced split is represented by arrow (4) in the money field (Figure O). The arrow shows money going into the expenses quadrant, some going into the asset quadrant, and some staying in the income quadrant.

Figure O

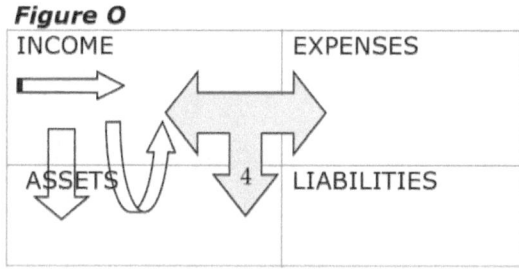

There is a psychological trick to never being broke, that is, always having money in your income quadrant. Don't allow yourself to go broke. Create a habit of always having money on your person.

If you are used to the application of the Money-in-Money-out rule, this may be strange and difficult at first, but it is the way to think about money effectively.

The classic statement in *The Richest Man in Babylon,* when personalized, says, "a part of all I earn is mine to keep". Are you a keeper or a spender? When do I start the Balanced Split rule? The answer is NOW! Some say, but my current system does not allow me any amount of money to be saved now.

I say, if going forward is what you would like to see happen in your life, then perhaps you should change your systems and make sure that you put yourself first. This may mean putting some that used to be first, last. This does not suggest being irresponsible, but it means adjusting and adapting.

The Spider-Web Economic Doctrine

Chika Onyeani, in his book, *Capitalist Nigger – The road to success*, introduces something he calls the spider-web economic doctrine applied by Asians in America to gain economic freedom. They create business networks such that all money that comes into such a network, never leaves the network. They build businesses of everything they need. Outsiders come and buy from them, but they never go and buy from outsiders.

They only spend their money within the network of businesses owned by one of them. This ensures that even their expenses, will come back as an income as whoever they bought from, will also come and buy from them. They understand the balanced split rule. They spend with ease because they have set up systems to ensure that the money, they spend will come back to them as an income.

> The spider web:
> When the owner of shop 1 wants an item, like clothing, they only buy from shop 2, and when the owner of shop 2 wants a car, they go to shop 3, who goes to shop 4 for some other item, etc. No one in the web buys anything outside this circle. This ensures that their money stays with the group, which forms a cartel.

SELF-ASSESSMENT

1. Explain the Pay-yourself-first rule

2. What is the spider-web economic doctrine?

3. Explain the balanced split rule

4. What are the benefits of paying yourself first?

Chapter 9

9. WHY IS IT DIFFICULT TO SAVE MONEY?

> "There is nothing we receive with so much reluctance as advice."
> Joseph Addison.

> LEARNING OUTCOMES
> In this chapter you will learn:
> 1. What makes savings so difficult
> 2. Problems related to lack of savings
> 3. Creating reasons for saving

The argument says, but saving doesn't work, I've done it for so many years and still I get to spend the money I have saved, I still have nothing to help me now, I have nothing to show for all my savings. It's one step forward, and two steps backwards.

Do you want to change? Would you like to effectively apply the Balanced Split rule?

George Clason said it best: a part of all I earn

is mine to keep. The keeping principle has been at the root of building wealth since money was invented.

It is only those that are able to keep money that are capacitated to build wealth. It does not matter how much you make; it matters how much you keep.

Those that are expert money spenders do not have a hope of building wealth. The worst are those who play the money game with other people's money, that is, borrowed money.

What are the reasons that many people can't practice the keeping principle? Many people's financial lives are unstructured. Everything is a surprise and therefore everything is an emergency. There is no forward thinking and there is no plan that is being followed. Even things that should not be a surprise are always a surprise including school fees and birthdays; and some people are in the habit of solving such "emergencies" by taking a loan, which creates other obvious problems of living for your creditors.

So, some of the problems are:

- *Lack of structure* in your finances will prevent you from being able to practice the keeping principle.
- *Lack of purpose or "reason why"*. Purpose creates motivation. Without a strong enough "Why", most people

never save! This means setting goals and targets for saving.

Saving money for no particular reason is not a good way to practice the keeping principle. You need to create a strong reason and motivation for saving.

- *Lack of proper financial planning*. Without a plan, you are shooting into the dark.
- *Ignorance of proper financial tools and instruments* that you can use to catapult you into a wealth builder.
  - ➢ If you choose to use the *stock market* as your tool, you must be informed of its intricacies so that you can derive maximum benefit from your efforts.
  - ➢ If you choose to use *real estate* as your tool, you have to know a lot about that sector.
  - ➢ If you choose *business*, you cannot be a scatterbrain that runs from business idea to business idea.
- *Sabotaging yourself* includes what we call stealing from yourself. You save for a particular purpose, like, to put down a deposit for a house, and then you divert the money to buy a car or to some other project unrelated to your initial purpose. That is self-sabotage. You are what Walt

Kelly's cartoon character Pogo meant when he said: "we have met they enemy, and he is us!"
- *Planning and not following your plan*. They say if you fail to plan, you have planned to fail. But then again, if you plan and do not follow through, you have also planned to fail.
- And of course, there are a lot of *disempowering beliefs* that make you think it is impossible to build wealth through savings! Check your beliefs.

The enemy could be right inside. It is time to change your mind about your capabilities!

The maxim from here on should be, "when money comes in, 'I will keep some and I will spend some'; or, 'a part of all I earn is mine to keep'.

For those who say, 'but I don't earn enough to save', I say, at this stage, it is not so much about how much you save, the most important thing is to start the habit of saving.

It is at this stage that some say: save for what? I can't save money when I have very little to live on!

The fact is, all purposeless saving will eventually disappear. If you save money but you have not assigned a specific task for it, some emergency will come and take it away.

- Find a purpose for your money, that is the only way you can keep it.
- Saving for an investment.
- Save it because you want some returns to come back to you.
- Save it because you want it to start working for you.
- Save it to start the new habit of saving. Our habits imprison us and the sooner we break the shackles off our feet, the sooner we can walk freely.

Savings have proved to be difficult for many of us because we see a saving as a thing that keeps you from enjoying your money. We also see saving as an end in itself instead of a means to an end.

The end is ROI (return on investments), not savings. When you save aimlessly, any pressure that comes will utilise your savings. But when you save with intent to invest, especially if that investment is important to you, then nothing will dissuade you from your path.

If you are saving money for a deposit on a house, then saving does not seem so difficult. If you are saving, just so that you can have money if an emergency comes, then the emergency almost always comes. All aimless savings end up nowhere. All purposeful savings lead to goal achievement. The application of the pay-yourself-first rule must be with intent to invest into some important project that will in turn produce satisfactory results for you.

The most important thing is to start the habit of saving!

SELF-ASSESSMENT

1. What has made saving money difficult? (list at least five reasons)

2. What are the good and viable reasons for saving money?

3. How can you start and sustain the habit of saving?

Chapter 10

10. DEBT AND FINANCIAL INTELLIGENCE

"I've been rich, and I've been poor; now that I know which is which, I'd rather be rich."
Dan Lee Dimke

> LEARNING OUTCOMES
>
> In this chapter you will learn:
> - How the financially intelligent borrow money
> - New conditions for borrowing money
> - The performing assets rule
> - The sponsoring rule
>
> Creating Security

Financial intelligence is not the domain of the rich only. Anyone who is willing to engage the rules, can benefit from all quadrants of the money game.

Do Financially Intelligent People Borrow Money?

A financially intelligent person does borrow money; but when she does, she makes sure of a few things. First, she does not borrow excessively for consumption, and if she can help it, she does not borrow for consumption at all.

When she does borrow for consumption, for example, as in credit card, she makes sure that she does not carry a balance on her credit card. This means whatever she charged on her credit card this month, gets paid off at the end of the month. Credit card companies only charge you interest on the balance left unpaid at the end of the month on your credit card. If you pay off everything you charged, you are essentially using their money for free.

Your reasons or motivation for borrowing money will go a long way in telling you about your relationship with your money, and other people's money. A financially intelligent person does not, as a general rule, borrow money without a full plan and debt strategy. She does not borrow money out of panic. She does not borrow money "for problems". She does not borrow money to repay debt.

If you say, okay, but I've made some financial mistakes. For example, I'm carrying a balance on my credit card, what do I do now? That's a good question.

This whole book works as a unit. The section on Debt management systems will come in handy. The key is to remain calm and not panic because it is very difficult to counsel panic. A person who is drowning tends to panic, but it is precisely remaining calm that could save that person's life. If you feel that you are drowning in debt, being calm right now may lead you to the most amicable solutions.

This is better than the irrational application of more debt to cover debt, thus perpetuating the problem.

4. Borrowing for Security

Let us address one of the most important concepts when it comes to borrowing money. Among the many advices that the richest man gave to his students in George Clason's *The Richest Man in Babylon* was this:

"make of thy dwelling a profitable investment"

Many a man spends too many years of their

working life paying exorbitant rentals to landlords. It is easy to think that it is cheaper to rent than to own. But because you are essentially losing time, in the long run, it proves to be more expensive to rent than to own. All that money that has gone to the landlord for all these years, could have gone towards the repayment of your own home loan.

It makes sense to buy or build your own home as a matter of priority. Creating security for yourself and your family is the first step towards freedom.

If you are going to borrow money, you can borrow for your home.

What does not make sense, however, is to spend twenty-five to thirty years paying for your first home. Yes, the lender said you can take up to thirty years to repay your mortgage. But don't forget that lenders are also players on the money field. The longer you take to repay this loan the more money they make off of you. Now, think about this. If you take that long to pay off your first home loan, when do you think, you will start focusing on other investments that will actually bring you an income? Your home will not bring you an income. It only gives you security. So, technically speaking, it is not an investment.

A career lasts for only forty years. If you start working at 20 to retire at 60, you only have 40 years. If you devote 30 years to paying off only one asset that will not bring in money, aren't you wasting time?

One of the things that prolongs home loan repayments are people who treat their house as if it's an ATM. They keep borrowing any extra equity from the home, reverting back to another 30 years.

The fact is, it is not impossible to pay off your home loan in 15 years or less. It does not even require that much more extra payments for you to achieve this. Look at the example below:

> Let's look at the numbers:
> If you borrowed one million (1'000'000), to repay it over 30 years (360 months), and you are charged say an interest of 11%p.a; your monthly repayments will be equal to 9'523.23.
> (Now, multiply the 9'523.23 by 360 months to see the total you will repay for your one million loan. The answer is: 3'428'362.80!) This mean the lender will make an extra 2,4million off of you.
> Now, what if you decided to sacrifice your entertainment money and added only 280.00 per month to your monthly home loan repayment?
> This means your repayments will now be 9'803.23.
> This will save you a full five years (60 months). You will have saved 488'025.00 in interest!
> If you decided to repay the same mortgage over 15 years instead of 30, your repayments will only be 11'365.96.

> The difference between 30 years and 15 years is only 1'842.73 per month!

This is the power of compound interest. Make it work in your favour instead of against you. Any self-respecting bank will have mortgage calculators on their website. You don't need to be an accountant to calculate this. Just go that website and enter the numbers and see. By just changing your repayment amount, you will see how much time it will take you. By just changing time, you will see how much more you have to repay. You don't even have to go to the bank's website; right there on your smart phone, you can search and download any mortgage calculator App.

5. Performing Assets Rule

When a financially intelligent person borrows money, they borrow for Performing Assets. A performing asset is an asset that makes money for you. A non-performing asset is an asset that does not make you money.

Your home, for example, is a non-performing asset. But it is a very crucial part of your asset base since it gives you security.

Borrowing for Performing Assets is represented by arrow (5) in the field below (Figure P). It is money coming from lenders (liabilities) but focusing on building an asset base.

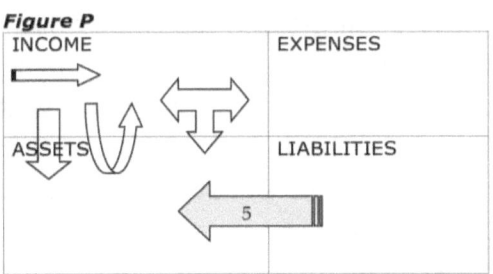

Figure P

This is the same movement that will happen when you borrow for security, that is, your primary home. Since you now know that the Repayment rule will come into play whenever you borrow money, as a financially intelligent person, you must be prepared for this.

For performing asset rule, the question financially intelligent people ask before they borrow money is: who is going to repay this loan? This will lead us to the next important consideration in the money game.

6. The Positive Cash Rule

The Positive cash rule says every time you

borrow money, it must generate positive cash, as opposed to negative cash. This means setting yourself up to make money from your loans.

Financially intelligent people therefore make sure that two things will be applicable in order to fulfil the positive cash rule:

1) The asset for which the loan was taken must be the kind of asset that can generate an income. The Income must be used to repay the loan;
2) It must also generate enough income into the income quadrant so that the borrower benefits from the loan.

On the money field (Figure Q), the first rule is represented by arrow (6).

This indicates that the money that repays the loan comes from the loan itself, or that the asset is generating income.

Let's look at the first rule of financially intelligent borrowing.

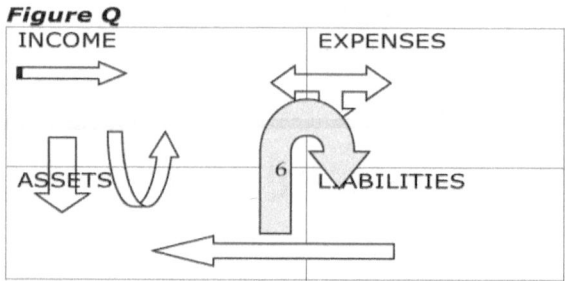

Figure Q

Whenever you borrow money, you make sure that you are not the one who is going to repay the loan.

An example of a performing asset for which you can borrow money and have this rule apply is real estate. If you borrowed money intelligently and purchased a rental property, that property should generate the cash to repay the loan.

7. The Profit rule or Income from liabilities rule

The second rule of borrowing is to ensure that, not only is the loan generating money to repay itself, but it must also generate money for you to benefit immediately from it. This is represented on the field (Figure R) by arrow (7), showing that your income is increasing as a direct function of the loan.

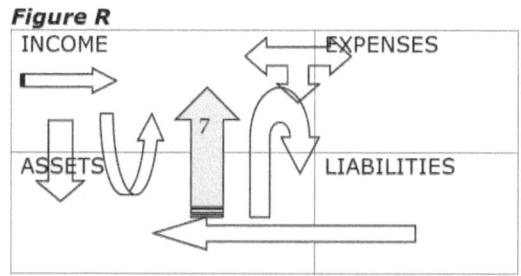

Figure R

The field below (Figure S), represents the three arrows all together. Arrows number 5, 6, and 7 must remain inextricably combined.

A performing asset loan (5) that creates cash to repay the loan (6), and a profit (7), is an intelligent loan.
The sum of arrows 6 and 7 represent positive cash flow.

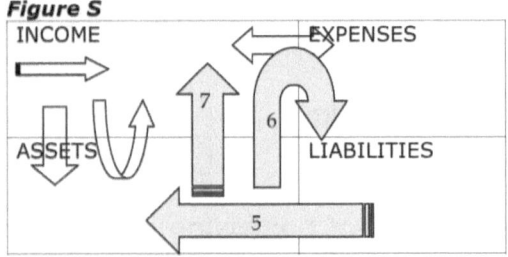

Figure S

8. The Sponsoring Rule

What most people do is they borrow money and buy a rental property. But because they don't do proper homework or understand the positive cash rule, the property becomes a burden on them.
Because the property does not generate enough money to repay the loan, they, out of

their salary, supplement the mortgage difference.

By so doing, you have just introduced a new rule in your money game: the sponsoring rule. What you are doing, in effect, is you are sponsoring someone to stay in your house.

If your mortgage repayment is 5 000.00, but your tenant is paying you 4 000.00 in rental, you are sponsoring your tenant by 1000.00. Your tenant is living a 5000.00 bucks' lifestyle but it's costing them only 4000.00, courtesy of you.

You are saying to your tenant: please come and stay in my house and I will pay an additional 1000.00 every month to supplement your lifestyle.

This is indicated by arrow (8) on the field (Figure T). It shows your own income supporting your liabilities. There is no arrow 7 (profit) as was in figure S.

This should never happen to financially intelligent people.

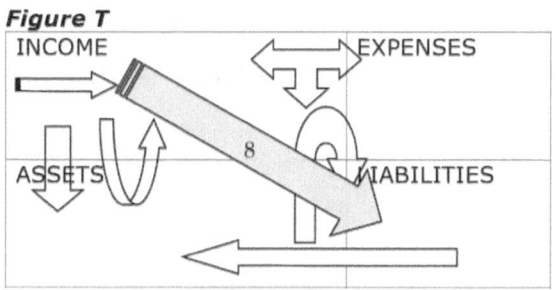

Figure T

This is what Robert Kiyosaki refers to when he asks the question: 'why would you knowingly lose money?' That is not financial intelligence. I am not saying that this is wrong or right.
All I am saying is, if that rental property was meant to be an investment, then you are having a negative return on your investments.

It is a pity that too many people do this and put forward other arguments to support this move. The most common argument is: but the property is appreciating in value. While that may be true, or not, the fact is, you are currently still sponsoring someone to stay in your house. As far as cash flow is concerned, you are not winning the game.
The second rule of borrowing money intelligently is to ensure that not only does the loan repay itself, but you too must benefit from the loan immediately. Simply put, the loan must generate positive cash flow.

Does my Income exceed my Expenses?

Using the rental property example, this means

that the rental received must exceed the expenses incurred.

The expenses are not just the loan repayment:
- Interest and capital; but other expenses such as:
- Insurance – both property insurance and credit life insurance
- Maintenance,
- Taxes and levies,
- Management fees, as well as a
- Provision for vacancy factor. The vacancy factor means, if the property should become vacant, there must be money put aside from the rentals in previous months to cover the months when you have no tenant. If you don't make this provision, it takes one month without a tenant for you to fall behind on your mortgage repayments. If this situation persists for say three to six months, you are in danger of losing your property to foreclosure or repossession.

This knowledge leads to financial intelligence.
Some might immediately say, properties that can produce those kinds of results are impossible to find.
Well, all the more reason to do your homework before you borrow money for such

investments.

If you play your game with knowledge and understanding, you will find that there are plenty of opportunities out there.

But if you play your game without knowledge of the rules and the intelligence to apply them, then you will believe that success is impossible. This is the difference between borrowing for consumption and borrowing for growth or for performing assets.

SELF-ASSESSMENT

1. How do financially intelligent people borrow money?

2. What are the two important rules to consider before borrowing money?

3. What is the sponsoring rule?

4. Why is it important to pay off your first mortgage faster?

Chapter 11

11. POSITIVE CASH FLOW AND RE-INVESTMENT

"If your outgo exceeds your income, your upkeep is your downfall"
Unknown

> **LEARNING OUTCOMES**
> In this chapter you will learn:
> - Performing Assets
> - Re-investing principles
> - Self-sustenance
> - The difference between good money field and dysfunctional money field

There are other performing assets for which you can borrow money and have the positive cash rule above apply. If you borrowed money for a viable and profitable business, then you make sure the business produces enough money to repay its own liabilities and leave you with a profit. Many people seem to understand that if you borrow money for a business, then the business must repay its own liabilities and give you a profit.

But many more people do not apply the same rule when they get into real estate. It may be primarily because they don't see real estate as a business, but the truth is, they should.

It is not just a long-term investment; it is a business that needs to make money almost immediately. You don't borrow money for a business and allow it to make a loss while you are sitting around arguing that your business is growing in value. It is either giving you a profit now, or it's not worth going into. What's the point of keeping a job to finance a business?

9. The Re-Investment Rule

The next question is: what do you do when money comes back into your income quadrant from your performing assets? Your primary purpose in this game should be to grow, not to shrink. When money comes into your income quadrant, whether through your savings or from other investments, you send it right back to the Asset quadrant so that it can generate more cash.

This is the Re-investment rule and is represented by arrow (9) on the money field (Figure U).

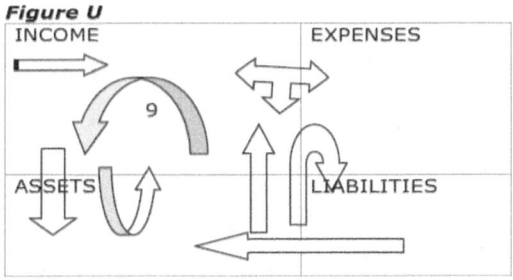
Figure U

This could arguably be the single most important rule on the money field that contributes to building wealth.

It is one thing to collect revenues; it is another thing to make profits, but it is quite another thing altogether to re-invest your profits.

At this stage some people might say, but that sounds miserly. I don't want to be stingy; I want to spend and enjoy my money now!

The answer is: if you want to enjoy your money without worry, then this is exactly what you need to create. You need to create a system that can continually generate cash for you to enjoy. That starts with re-investing for growth. For a lot of people, the only source of income is their job. They have nothing else to help them. I am not talking here about saving money forever and never getting to enjoy your money.

I am talking here about creating a system that can help you generate more cash for your enjoyment.

10. The Self-sustenance rule

The self-sustenance rule is about building a system from which you can continue to live. When this system is set up, you will see how a financially intelligent person can start spending money. Not only from the meagre salary, but most or all of your expenses can start coming from your asset quadrant. Arrow (10) in Figure V shows that assets can support expenses.

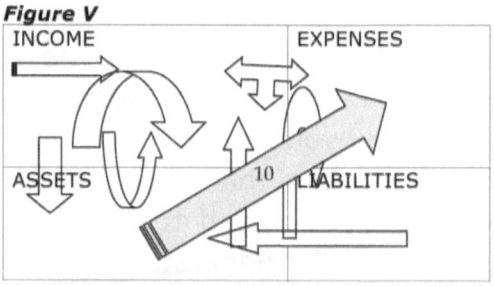

Figure V

This is what financial freedom is all about. It is about creating a system that can help you with your living expenses without you labouring hard for it.

Sure, it takes time to set up such a system, but it surely can be set up. Financial freedom is about systems. It is not the amount of money coming in, whether little or too much, it is a system that can keep it coming in whether you work it or not.

This is what is referred to as passive income. The river may start off as a trickle, and then it becomes a creek, and then a mighty river with lots of fish swimming your way. Now you have a system that can support you in all seasons.

Figure W
THE FINANCIAL GREEN LINE:

The above money field represents all the arrows on the field:
1. The Income rule
2. The pay yourself first rule
3. The return-on-investment rule
4. The balanced split rule
5. The borrowing for security and performing assets rule
6. The Positive Cash flow rule

7. The Income from liabilities rule or The Profit rule
8. (We skip the sponsoring rule since it is not a rule applied by the financially intelligent)
9. The re-investment rule
10. The self-sustenance rule

Now, compare this with the LIFE-STYLE focused diagram that we discussed in chapter five (replicated below) and choose.

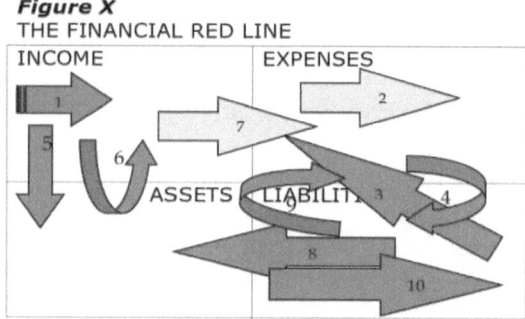

Figure X
THE FINANCIAL RED LINE

The Life-Style focused diagram is bleeding your resources. It is bleeding you to the ground. It is what we call the financial red line!

The Wealth-Style focused diagram is meant to help you grow. It is a breeding life, instead of a bleeding life. If you notice, Figure X, The Financial Red Line, shows that the play is mostly on the right side of the money field. The flow of money is focused on *expenses and liabilities*. This is the lifestyle focused diagram. The diagram on the intelligent money field

(Figure W) is focused on the left side of the money field, or on _income and assets_. This is the wealth-style focused diagram.

So, the question is are you focused on building a lifestyle or are you focused on building wealth?

The Re-investment Rule could arguably be the most important rule of wealth building

SELF-ASSESSMENT

1. What question do financial intelligent people consider before borrowing money, and which money rule requires them to ask this question?

2. What is the re-investment rule?

3. What is the difference between the life style focus and the wealth building cycle?

Chapter 12

12. FINANCIAL GOALS

"Becoming an expert at goal setting and goal achieving is something that you absolutely must do if you wish to fulfil your potential as a human being".
Brian Tracy

LEARNING OUTCOMES
In this chapter you will learn:
- Why people do not set goals
- Why it's important to write down goals
- How to successfully set goals
- SMART Goals

Success Through Goal Setting

Brian Tracy, quoted above, has written more than 36 books and produced more than 300 audio and video learning programs, including the "Psychology of Achievement."

Let's look at some excerpts from some of his writings on Goal Setting. Goals enable you, among other things, to do the work you want to do, and to become the kind of person you want to be.

Yet, writes Tracy, according to the best research, less than 3% of people have written goals, and less than 1% review and rewrite their goals on a daily basis.

Why do so few people set goals? Here are a few basic reasons.

1. **They are simply not serious.** In other words, until you become completely serious and determined about your goals, nothing really happens.
2. **They don't understand the importance of goals.** As Zig Zigler says: "Most people don't plan to fail, but there are many failures because people fail to plan." Until you have a goal, you have nothing to achieve. The plan hinges on the goal.
3. **They don't know how to do it. Brian Tracy writes:** "One of the greatest tragedies of our educational system is that you can receive 15 to 18 years of education and never once receive a single hour of instruction on how to set goals."
4. **Fear. Fear of rejection. Fear of criticism. Fear of ostracism. Fear of**

failure. People often hold back from setting worthwhile goals because every time they do set a goal, somebody steps up and tells them that they can't achieve it, or that they will lose their money or waste their time. **Fear of failure** is probably the greatest single obstacle to success in adult life. It can hold you back more than any other psychological problem. What would you do if you were not afraid?

If you can overcome obstacles and set well-defined goals, you can channel your efforts and focus your energy toward something important to you.
Goal setting gives you a target to aim at and enables you to develop the self-discipline to continue working toward your target rather than becoming distracted and going off in other directions.
When you look around you, you will see that all achievement is the triumph of persistence.
You will see people everywhere who are struggling with, and overcoming adversities in order to accomplish something that is important to them. And so can you.

The Power of Writing Down Your Goals

Studies show that people who put their goals down on paper have a much higher level of achievement than those who don't.

If you want to be a high achiever, write down your goals – and read them repeatedly.

According to Tom Bay, in his book entitled *Look Within or Do Without*, Harvard Business School did a study on the financial status of its students 10 years after graduation. The Study found that:

- As many as 27% of them needed financial assistance.
- A whopping 60% of them were living paycheque to paycheque (that is, hand to mouth survival)
- A mere 10% of them were living comfortably.
- And only 3% of them were financially independent.

The study also looked at goal setting and found these interesting correlations:

- The 27% that needed financial assistance had absolutely no goal setting processes in their lives.
- The 60% that were living pay-cheque

- to pay-cheque had basic survival goals (such as managing to live pay-cheque to pay-cheque).
- The 10% that were living comfortably had general goals. They thought they knew where they were going to be in the next five years.
- The 3% that were financially independent had written out their goals and the steps required to reach those goals.

Well, what do you do with statistics such as these? Do you say, well, they seem too perfectly correlated perhaps just to make a point, or do you consider that there is merit in these findings?

While many of us have the degree, we did not get the education, and it does not matter what school you went to.

The real school is in the "University of Hard-knocks", called real life. Why would writing down goals make the difference? Why can't I just think generally about them?

Number one, writing creates a focus. When you actually have to come up with descriptive words to represent the picture you have in your mind, more questions about how you will achieve that will surface and you will have to answer them, and that provides you with clarity.

Secondly, once you get clarity, it may take you

away from fantasyland and bring you down to the practicality of your desires. If you say I want to have a million bucks within a year, writing that down may bring you to ask, how much do I have to make per month, per week, per day? That will paint a different picture because now you have to face what is possible.

Smart Goals

Keep your goals SMART. This is an acronym that will help you in setting your goals.

S = Specific – not general like I want to be rich, but how much do you want to be worth? You have to get specific in all areas of your finances.
How much of your debt do you want to have paid by when? How much savings do you want to accumulate by when? How much sales do you want to achieve by when?

M = Measurable – can you break them down? What is the unit of measure? What currency? How many units of sales per period?

A = Achievable – can other people of equal ability and skill, given the same opportunity,

achieve them.
Achievability helps you to keep your head out of the clouds and out of fantasyland.
- Are there specific actions that can be taken to achieve this goal?
- Are you capable of doing this?
- Do you have the skills to achieve this?

List the skills or the tools it will take to achieve this.

R = Realistic – not pie in the sky; Can you match the specific skills that you have with this goal. (Not dependent on factors over which you have no control)
If you say I want to be a bestselling author; the first question is, can you write? The second question is, can you sell? The third question is, can you write a sellable book? The next question is, are you willing to do both – that is, write a sellable book and get out and sell it? Another question would be, are there readily available systems that you can follow to do this? As you can see, "realism", is brought about by a series of connected questions that need to be answered. Nothing should be left to chance.

T = Timely – set a timeline. Making a million within a year implies that each month you will have average revenue of not less than

83 333.33; which breaks down to a further 20 833.33 per week on average, which breaks down to a further average of 4 166.67 per day. Now you can go back and ask yourself the preceding questions such as, is this realistic and achievable? Should I reduce the goal to half a million or should I increase the time to two years?

For each goal that you have, see if it can fit the mould as set out in the next page.

	GOALS AND DETAILS
SPECIFIC	
MEASURABLE	
ACHIEVABLE	
REALISTIC	
TIMELY	

Set your goals for each quadrant of the money field.

INCOME GOALS	EXPENSES GOALS
ASSET GOALS	LIABILITIES GOALS

SELF-ASSESSMENT

1. Why is it important to set goals?

2. How can you effectively set goals?

3. What are SMART goals?

ACKNOWLEDGEMENTS

The recreation of this book series was as a result of the revision of *Functional Mastery Over My Finances*. We created a course that got accredited by Botswana Qualifications Authority (BQA). We needed a more relevant "text book" that could accompany the course.

Once I had ploughed through the material, my colleague and fellow personal finance educator Poloko Mongatane was a great help in not only pushing for the accreditation of the course, but getting her hands dirty and helping to create some of the assessment questions at the end of some of the chapters, as well as doing some editing.

All this was supposed to be one big book. In fact, the paperback version remains one book divided into three parts. The book series idea however came in a bit to reduce the book to chewable chunks instead of one big bite.

Great thanks to all the people who have given feedback since the publication of the first book in 2008. Many thanks also to all the workshop participants who brought in new perspectives on some of the concepts and for helping to improve them.

Many thanks to my staff at Moedi Financial Training for their constant support. Oteng "Owty" Orakanye, many of the workshops that have happened to improve this material would not have happened without you.

My gratitude goes to my family always for their unending support.

Thank you

Nelson Letshwene

ABOUT THE AUTHOR

Nelson Letshwene is a Financial Planner, a professional speaker, and the author of several books including *Faith and Purpose – Living Life to the full without Fear, Guilt, or Regrets*. He is also the author of *Your Longing Is Your Calling – Finding your Purpose through the seven desires of life*.

He holds a bachelors degree in business economics from The University of the Witwatersrand (Wits) (Johannesburg), an Honours degree from The University of South Africa (UNISA), and a Post Graduate Diploma in Financial Planning from Milpark Education.

He is a speaker on Financial and Functional literacy issues. He has written for several newspapers and magazines on personal finance issues. He has hosted several radio shows focusing on personal finance.

For more please visit his website on

www.nelsonletshwene.com

Or his Money Skills blog on

www.7moneyskills.wordpress.com

Like his facebook page and You Tube channel, called:
Money Skills with Nelson Letshwene

BIBLIOGRAPHY

1. Abraham Jay, 1995, 2002, 9 Pillars to business growth, Torrance, CA, Abraham Publishing group, Inc.
2. Berger Rob, Top 100 Money Quotes of all time, www.forbes.com
3. Cameron, B. 2003. Getting Started: Money Matters for Under 25s. Cape Town: Zebra Press
4. Cameron, B. 2003. Massive fraud in funeral assurance industry exposed. Personal Finance: 1, August 9.
5. Cameron, B. 2003. Steep rise in lapsed policies. Personal Finance:1. September 27.
6. Clark, J.B. 1990. Marketing Today – Successes, Failures, and Turnarounds, 2nd eds. New Jersey: Prentice-Hall Inc.
7. Clason George S, 1926, The Richest Man in Babylon, Penguin books
8. Griffin, G. Edward, 1994, The Creature from Jekyll Island, American Media
9. Hill, Napolean, 1937, Think and Grow Rich, Fawcett books, New York
10. Johnson, S. Et al. 1999. Saving Faith. Boston: DPI
11. Kiyosaki, R.T and Lechter, S.L 1997. Rich Dad Poor Dad, - what the rich teach their kids about money that the poor and middle class do not. New York, Warner Books Inc.
12. Kiyosaki, R.T and Lechter, S.L 1999. Cashflow Quadrant, New York, Warner Books Inc
13. Kiyosaki, R.T and Lechter, S.L 2000. Rich Dad's Guide to becoming rich, without cutting up your credit

cards. New York. Warner Audio Books.
14. Kiyosaki, R.T and Lechter, S.L 2000. Rich Dad's Guide to Investing. New York. Warner Books.
15. Kiyosaki, R.T and Lechter, S.L 2001-2005, The Business School, 2nd ed, Momentum Media.
16. Kiyosaki, R.T and Lechter, S.L 2008, Increase Your Financial IQ, New York, Business Plus
17. Landsburg, Steven, E, 1993, The Armchair Economist, Simon & Schuster, London
18. Langemeier, Loral, 2005, The Millionaire Maker, McGraw-Hill
19. Langemeier, Loral, 2007, The Millionaire Maker's Guide to creating a Cash Machine for life, McGraw-Hill
20. Langemeier, Loral, 2009, Put More Cash in your Pocket: Turn what you know into dough, Harper Paperbacks
21. Lechter, M, Other People's Money, Warner Books, New York
22. Letshwene, R.N, 2008, Functional Mastery Over My Finances, Reach Publishers
23. Letshwene, R.N. 2004, UNISA, Personal Financial Management in Botswana
24. Letshwene, R.N. 2010, The Retirement Report, Moedi Publishing, Gaborone
25. Letshwene, R.N. 2011, Mastery Over Debt (Audio) Moedi Publishing, Gaborone
26. Letshwene, R.N. 2013, The Savings Report, Moedi Publishing, Gaborone
27. Masterson, M. 2005. Automatic Wealth – the 6 steps to financial independence. New Jersey: John Wiley & Sons Inc.
28. Orman, S. 2001. The Road to Wealth- a comprehensive guide to your money.

29. Orman, S. 2003. The Laws of Money, the lessons of life. New York. Simon & Schuster Inc. (Audio book)
30. Patel, Raj, 2009, The Value of Nothing, Portobello books.
31. Stanley Thomas, J, and Danko William, D, 1996, The Millionaire Next Door, Pocket Books, New York
32. Swart, N.J. 2003, Personal Financial Management, the Southern African guide to personal financial planning, 2nd Edition, Lansdowne: Juta
33. Swart, N.J. 2003, Starting and buying your own business in a franchise, Cape Town: Juta
34. Wilde Stuart, 1989, The Trick to Money is having some!, Hay House, London
35. Hartmann Thom, The Last Hours of Ancient Sunlight, Three Rivers Press, NY, 2004
36. www.Investopedia.com

RECOMMENDED READING

1. Ask and it is given, by Esther and Jerry Hicks (Hay House)
2. Born Rich by Bob Proctor
3. Conversations with God , by Neale Donald Walsch
4. Personal Financial Mastery, by Nelson Letshwene (audio program)
5. Rich Dad Poor Dad, by Robert Kiyosaki
6. The Millionaire Maker, Loral Langemeier
7. The One minute millionaire, by Robert Allen & Mark Victor Hansen
8. The Richest Man in Babylon, by George Clason
9. The Science of Getting Rich, by Wallace D. Wattles
10. The Strangest Secret, by Earl Nightingale (audio program)
11. Think and Grow Rich, by Napoleon Hill
12. The Millionaire Next Door, by Thomas j Stanly and William D Danko

For Other Books by NELSON LETSHWENE

SCAN THIS

Or go to:

www.amazon.com/R-Nelson-Letshwene/e/B00Q4AEMCM/ref

Nelson Letshwene

THANK YOU

If you enjoyed reading this book, please feel free to leave me a review on amazon.com. Reviews help other readers to know the relevance of the book for them and they help authors like me to improve on our work for the benefit of our readers.

Nelson Letshwene

www.ingramcontent.com/pod-product-compliance
Lightning Source LLC
Chambersburg PA
CBHW020426220526
45464CB00002B/589